A Guide to
AMERICAN STATES

D0386213

Pennsylvania

THE KEYSTONE STATE

www.av2books.com

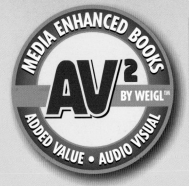

AV² provides enriched content that supplements and complements this book. Weigl's AV² books strive to create inspired learning and engage young minds in a total learning experience.

Your AV² Media Enhanced books come alive with...

Audio
Listen to sections of the book read aloud.

Key Words
Study vocabulary, and complete a matching word activity.

Video
Watch informative video clips.

Quizzes
Test your knowledge.

Embedded Weblinks
Gain additional information for research.

Slide Show
View images and captions, and prepare a presentation.

Try This!
Complete activities and hands-on experiments.

... and much, much more!

Go to **www.av2books.com**, and enter this book's unique code.

BOOK CODE

S647484

AV² by Weigl brings you media enhanced books that support active learning.

Published by AV² by Weigl
350 5th Avenue, 59th Floor
New York, NY 10118
Website: www.av2books.com   www.weigl.com

Library of Congress Cataloging-in-Publication Data

Evdokimoff, Natasha.
 Pennsylvania / Natasha Evdokimoff.
     p. cm. -- (A guide to American states)
 Includes index.
 ISBN 978-1-61690-810-2 (hardcover : alk. paper) -- ISBN 978-1-61690-486-9 (online)
 1. Pennsylvania--Juvenile literature. I. Title.
 F149.3.E932 2011
 974.8--dc23
                      2011019030

Printed in the United States of America in North Mankato, Minnesota

052011
WEP180511

Project Coordinator Jordan McGill
Art Director Terry Paulhus

Photo Credits
Every reasonable effort has been made to trace ownership and to obtain permission to reprint copyright material. The publishers would be pleased to have any errors or omissions brought to their attention so that they may be corrected in subsequent printings.

Weigl acknowledges Getty Images as its primary image supplier for this title.

3 1907 00288 8054

Contents

AV² Book Code 2

Introduction 4

Where Is Pennsylvania? 6

Mapping Pennsylvania 8

The Land 10

Climate 12

Natural Resources 14

Plants 16

Animals 18

Tourism 20

Industry 22

Goods and Services 24

American Indians 26

Explorers 28

Early Settlers 30

Notable People 32

Population 34

Politics and Government 36

Cultural Groups 38

Arts and Entertainment 40

Sports 42

National Averages Comparison 44

How to Improve My Community 45

Exercise Your Mind! 46

Words to Know / Index 47

Log on to www.av2books.com 48

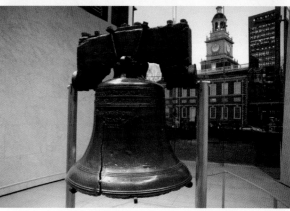

Both the Declaration of Independence and the U.S. Constitution were signed at Independence Hall in Philadelphia.

Introduction

Pennsylvania means "Penn's woodland." It is named for William Penn, the English Quaker who founded a colony there in 1682. Pennsylvania's nickname is the Keystone State. The nickname represents the state's central role in the formation of the United States. It also reflects Pennsylvania's central location among the original 13 colonies.

The state has a rich political history. During the American Revolution, Pennsylvania was the center of action. The Declaration of Independence was approved in Philadelphia on July 4, 1776, in the Pennsylvania State House. That building is now called Independence Hall.

Forbes *magazine ranked Pittsburgh as the nation's "most livable city."*

Lancaster County is the heart of Pennsylvania's Amish community.

Later, a famous Civil War battle was fought in Pennsylvania. The Battle of Gettysburg in 1863 was an important victory for the Union. As a result of heavy losses at Gettysburg, the Southern states that made up the Confederacy would never again be able to launch a major attack against the North.

Modern-day Pennsylvania is productive and diverse. State residents work in a wide variety of occupations, from farming to high-technology industries. In addition to its many historical sites and museums, the state features beautiful countryside and colorful folkways that make Pennsylvania a magnet for tourists. With more than 1.5 million residents, Philadelphia is the state's leading **urban** center and one of the largest cities in the United States. Pittsburgh ranks second in the state, with a population of more than 300,000 people.

Where Is Pennsylvania?

Pennsylvania is in the Middle Atlantic region of the United States. It is bordered by the states of New York to the north and New Jersey to the east. Delaware and Maryland are to the south. West Virginia borders Pennsylvania in the southwest, and Ohio in the west. Water boundaries are formed by the Delaware River on the eastern edge of the state and Lake Erie on the northwest.

Opened to traffic in 1940, the Pennsylvania Turnpike was the nation's first superhighway. It was called the "tunnel highway" because vehicles had to drive through seven tunnels as the highway crossed the mountainous landscape of central and western Pennsylvania. Today, the Pennsylvania Turnpike system extends more than 500 miles, with the main section forming part of east-west Interstate 76, or I-76.

The Benjamin Franklin Bridge spans the Delaware River, connecting Philadelphia with Camden, New Jersey.

Other major interstate highways that cross Pennsylvania include I-80 and I-78, which run east-west, and I-81 and I-75, which run north-south.

The major air terminals in the state are Philadelphia International Airport and Pittsburgh International Airport. Amtrak provides the state with passenger rail service, and both Philadelphia and Pittsburgh have rapid-transit systems that link the cities with their suburbs.

Amtrak's Acela express train takes less than two hours to travel between downtown Philadelphia and Washington, D.C.

At the peak of construction, work crews built the Pennsylvania Turnpike at a rate of 3.5 miles per day.

I DIDN'T KNOW THAT!

Mason and Dixon's Line, which was considered the boundary between the North and the South, defines the border that Pennsylvania shares with Maryland. It was established in 1769.

The state seal is a shield depicting a ship, a plow, and bundles of wheat. Above it sits an eagle.

The state flag bears the official coat of arms on a background of dark blue.

The state motto, "Virtue, Liberty and Independence," first appeared on a Pennsylvania coat of arms in the late 1700s. The motto was not officially adopted until 1875.

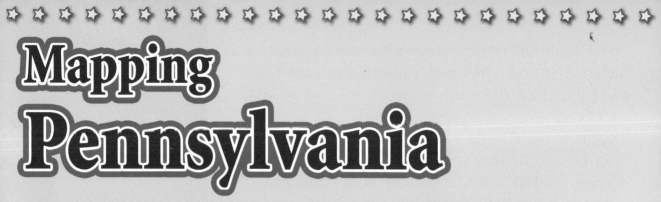

Mapping Pennsylvania

Rectangular in shape, Pennsylvania occupies a total area of 46,055 square miles. Land makes up about 97 percent of the total, and water accounts for the remaining 3 percent. Pennsylvania's share of Lake Erie makes up more than half of the state's water area. In total area, the state ranks 33rd in size among all the states. Railroads provide freight service and also allow for passenger trains.

Sites and Symbols

STATE SEAL
Pennsylvania

STATE BIRD
Ruffed Grouse

STATE FLOWER
Mountain Laurel

STATE FLAG
Pennsylvania

STATE ANIMAL
White-tailed Deer

STATE TREE
Hemlock

Nickname The Keystone State

Motto Virtue, Liberty and Independence

Song "Pennsylvania," words and music by Eddie Khoury and Ronnie Bonner

Entered the Union December 12, 1787, as the 2nd state

Capital Harrisburg

Population (2010 Census) 12,702,379

Ranked 6th state

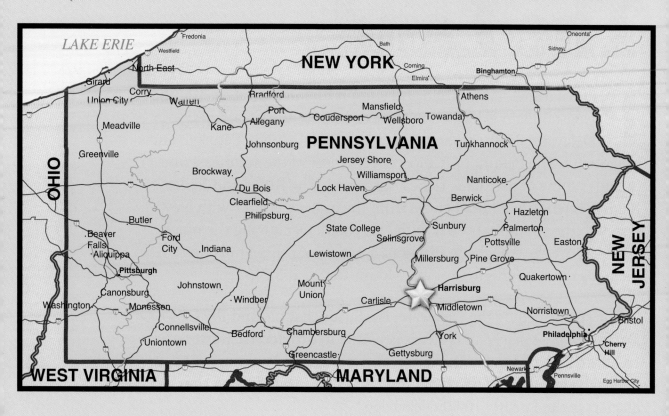

LAKE ERIE

NEW YORK

PENNSYLVANIA

OHIO

NEW JERSEY

WEST VIRGINIA

MARYLAND

STATE CAPITAL

Philadelphia and Lancaster served as Pennsylvania's state capital until Harrisburg became the seat of government in 1812. Centrally located on the Susquehanna River, Harrisburg has long been a hub of transportation and commerce for the state. Today, the city has a population of about 47,000.

N

Map Scale

0   50 Miles

LEGEND	
—	Road
—	River
☆	State Capital
•	City
▢	Pennsylvania
▬	State Border

United States

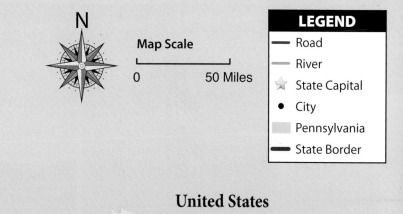

Hawai'i Alaska

Pennsylvania

The Land

Pennsylvania has a varied and complex landscape. The Atlantic Coastal Plain is located in the extreme southeast, along the Delaware River **estuary**. It includes Philadelphia, Pennsylvania's largest city. The Piedmont Region covers most of the southeast and includes some of the state's richest farmland. The Ridge and Valley Region extends in a broad curve from the eastern border with New Jersey to the southern border with Maryland. Occupying the north and west are the Allegheny Plateaus, a region of rolling hills that includes the state's highest point, Mount Davis, at 3,213 feet.

Major rivers include the Delaware, the Susquehanna, and the Ohio. Dams along Pennsylvania's rivers generate **hydroelectric power** and create artificial lakes for recreation and storage of drinking water. Pennsylvania also has many natural lakes that formed when the glaciers melted nearly 10,000 years ago.

LAKE ERIE

With a maximum depth of 210 feet, Lake Erie is the shallowest of the Great Lakes.

SUSQUEHANNA RIVER

Extending through the central part of the state, the Susquehanna River provides water for drinking, electric power, and recreation.

ALLEGHENY NATIONAL FOREST

Established in 1923, Allegheny National Forest covers 513,325 acres.

RICKETTS GLEN STATE PARK

More than 20 waterfalls highlight the 7.2-mile Falls Trail through the Glens Natural Area of Ricketts Glen State Park.

The Allegheny National Forest is the only national forest in Pennsylvania. It has about 200 miles of hiking trails and more than 50 miles of ski trails.

More than 34 million people each year visit Pennsylvania's more than 100 state parks.

Pittsburgh is located where the Allegheny and Monongahela rivers meet to form the Ohio River. Waters from the Ohio River pass through Pennsylvania and eventually drain into the Gulf of Mexico.

Groundhog Day traditions in Punxsutawney date back more than 125 years. Legend has it that if the groundhog Punxsutawney Phil sees his shadow on the morning of February 2, there will be six more weeks of winter. If he does not, people can expect an early spring.

Climate

T he climate in Pennsylvania is humid with plenty of rainfall. The southeastern part of the state enjoys long summers and mild winters, while the uplands to the north have short summers and harsh winters. Statewide, temperatures in the summer average about 70° Fahrenheit. In the winter months the average temperature is about 30° F. The record high temperature for the state is 111° F, set in Phoenixville in 1936. The all-time low is –42° F, set in Smethport in 1904. Cold winter winds that blow over the warmer waters of Lake Erie produce "lake effect snow," dumping an average of more than 80 inches of snow annually on the city of Erie.

Average Annual Temperatures Across Pennsylvania

Temperatures in Philadelphia tend to be warmer than in other Pennsylvania cities. What geographical factors account for this difference?

Degrees Fahrenheit

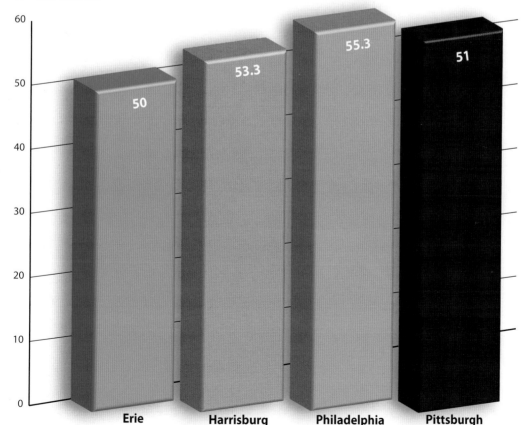

Natural Resources

Early settlers relied on the state's fertile farmland and extensive forests. Today, forests cover nearly 27,000 square miles in the state, and farms occupy more than 12,000 square miles. Fuels and other minerals are also important to the state economy. Pennsylvania is one of the nation's leading producers of crushed stone and cement. Annual production of all nonfuel minerals is worth about $2 billion.

Lancaster County, in southeastern Pennsylvania, has more than 5,400 farms. Sales of crops and livestock produced in the county total more than $1 billion annually.

Coal mines have operated in the state for more than 200 years, supplying energy for factories and heat for homes. Although Pennsylvania's coal industry has declined in recent decades, the state still provides about 5 percent of the nation's coal supply. Coal-powered generators produce about half of the state's electricity. Another 35 percent of Pennsylvania's electricity comes from nuclear power. Oil has been produced in the state for more than 150 years. New drilling methods are expected to bring a major increase in natural gas output.

The world's first commercial oil well was drilled in Titusville in 1859.

Limestone, commonly found in Pennsylvania, is used to make cement.

The worst nuclear accident in U.S. history took place at the Three Mile Island power plant near Harrisburg in 1979. No injuries were reported, although the plant experienced a near-meltdown.

Mining of anthracite coal began in northeastern Pennsylvania in 1775. Anthracite, also called hard coal, is one of the purest, cleanest-burning forms of coal.

Plants

About 60 percent of Pennsylvania is forested. White pine, beech, and sugar maple trees are found in the north. White oak, chestnut, and hickory trees are found in the south. Pennsylvania's state tree is the hemlock.

Cranberries flourish in Pennsylvania's marshy areas, and blueberry bushes grow well on the state's rocky hillsides. Flowers are also plentiful. Colorful violets, mountain laurels, and lady's slippers grow across the state.

HEMLOCK

Although hemlock trees grow in every Pennsylvania county, they are most commonly found in mountainous areas of the state.

CHESTNUT TREE

Chestnut trees dominated Pennsylvania forests until disease wiped out many of them. Forestry experts are working hard to restore the state's chestnut population.

BLUEBERRIES

Prized by birds and other wildlife, lowbush blueberries grow wild throughout the state.

MOUNTAIN LAUREL

Mountain laurel, the state flower, blooms in Pennsylvania from late May to mid-June.

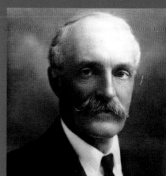

Animals

Pennsylvania's extensive woodlands provide shelter for many animals. Raccoons, squirrels, rabbits, skunks, and woodchucks are common. Deer, black bears, and coyotes also make their home in the forests. Lakes and rivers are well-stocked with fish. Trout, perch, pike, bass, and catfish swim in state waters.

The Keystone State is home to many kinds of birds. Birdwatchers can view robins, cardinals, and mockingbirds. The state bird is the ruffed grouse. Its reddish-brown color makes it easy for this bird to hide undetected in bushes.

WHITE-TAILED DEER

Overhunting and loss of habitat drastically reduced the number of deer in Pennsylvania by the end of the 19th century. Since then, efforts by conservationists have helped the deer population to rebound.

RACCOON

Raccoons are found throughout the state, especially near rivers, streams, and lakes. They eat a wide variety of foods and prefer to make their dens among hardwood trees.

RUFFED GROUSE

Because of changes in forest habitat, Pennsylvania's grouse population has declined by 30 to 50 percent since the early 1980s.

BROOK TROUT

To promote sport fishing and a healthy aquatic habitat, the government maintains fish hatcheries throughout the state. It annually stocks Pennsylvania lakes and streams with more than 3 million trout.

The brook trout is the state fish.

The crest of the state seal is an eagle, which is a symbol of strength and purity.

The white-tailed deer is the state animal.

The firefly, also known as the lightning bug, became the state insect in 1974.

The Great Dane is the state dog. Pennsylvania's early settlers used Great Danes as hunting dogs.

The largest striped bass caught in Pennsylvania waters weighed more than 53 pounds. Other record catches include a muskellunge weighing more than 54 pounds and a flathead catfish of more than 48 pounds.

Tourism

Visitors to Pennsylvania spend more than $30 billion per year. One of the state's major tourist attractions is the Liberty Bell at Independence National Historical Park in Philadelphia. The Liberty Bell has been rung on many historic occasions.

National military parks also attract tourists to the Keystone State, including the Valley Forge and Gettysburg parks. Led by General George Washington, troops from the 13 colonies camped at Valley Forge during the American Revolution. At the Battle of Gettysburg in July 1863, Union troops halted a Confederate invasion of the North in a three-day battle.

People also visit the farm region known as "Pennsylvania Dutch" country. In this region, visitors can observe the Amish way of life. The Amish actually are of German rather than Dutch ancestry. They seek to live a simple, **rural** life without relying on modern technology.

LIBERTY BELL

The Liberty Bell and other Independence National Historical Park attractions receive more than 3.7 million visitors per year.

THRILL RIDES

Pennsylvania amusement parks include Knoebels in the Poconos, Sesame Place and Hersheypark in the southeast, and Kennywood near Pittsburgh.

GETTYSBURG

More than 1,300 monuments, markers, and memorials at Gettysburg National Military Park honor those who fought in the Civil War.

POCONO RACEWAY

The Pocono 500 and Pennsylvania 500 are highlights of NASCAR's summer season.

Industry

After Europeans arrived, lumber was Pennsylvania's first major industry. Loggers cut down trees for wood to build settlements and ships. When forests began to decline, lumber production was nearly stopped. Recent **reforestation** has revived the lumber industry.

Industries in Pennsylvania
Value of Goods and Services in Millions of Dollars

For much of Pennsylvania's history, resource-based industries such as lumber and steel dominated the state economy. Today, the health-care industry accounts for one-tenth of Pennsylvania's economy, a higher proportion than in many other states. What might the size of the health-care industry indicate about the average age of the population in Pennsylvania?

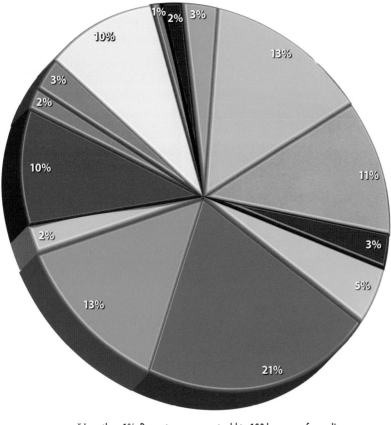

LEGEND

* Agriculture, Forestry, and Fishing $2,440
- Mining. $4,630
- Utilities $10,752
- Construction $19,157
- Manufacturing $68,486
- Wholesale and Retail Trade $61,652
- Transportation $16,197
- Media and Entertainment $25,599
- Finance, Insurance, and Real Estate $117,524
- Professional and Technical Services $72,182
- Education $11,909
- Health Care $55,056
- Hotels and Restaurants $11,793
- Other Services $14,042
- Government $56,446

TOTAL $547,865

* Less than 1%. Percentages may not add to 100 because of rounding.

Iron and steel production was Pennsylvania's main industry for many years. By the Civil War, Johnstown had the largest steel plant in the United States, and Pennsylvania was the leading supplier of steel for the Union armies. Today, the steel industry has shrunk because of foreign competition. Many thousands of Pennsylvania steelworkers have been forced to find new jobs. Even so, Pennsylvania remains one of the nation's leading steel-producing states.

Electronics and related fields have now taken over as Pennsylvania's major manufacturing sector. The state is a top manufacturer of computer parts and high-technology systems. Medicine is another important industry. Prescription drugs are made in the state for use around the world.

I DIDN'T KNOW THAT!

The Conestoga wagon was developed in Lancaster County around 1750. The wagon could carry up to six tons of passengers and cargo.

Pennsylvania's first newspaper was the *American Weekly Mercury*, founded in Philadelphia in 1719.

Manufacturing industries employ more than 550,000 people in Pennsylvania.

A U.S. Mint is located in Philadelphia. Visitors to the Mint can see official U.S. coins being made.

Pennsylvania produces more than 6 million tons of raw steel per year and is a leader in the production of stainless steel.

Goods and Services

The soil in Pennsylvania is fertile and ideal for many crops. Some Pennsylvania farms raise livestock, while others grow grains and vegetables. Dairy farms are most common in the northern part of the state.

Dairy items such as milk and cheese are some of the state's most important agricultural products. Other farm products include poultry, eggs, corn, potatoes, mushrooms, beans, and wheat. Winter wheat, which is used to make fine pastry and cake flour, is an important crop in Pennsylvania's southeast. Buckwheat, which does not need a long growing season, is an important northeastern crop.

The Hershey Company is the nation's largest chocolate maker. The company also operates Hershey's Chocolate World, a major tourist attraction.

Dairy farms in Pennsylvania have more than 540,000 cows and produce more than 10 billion pounds of milk annually.

Pennsylvania also grows a variety of fruits. Apples and peaches are raised on southeastern mountain slopes. Cherries, apples, and grapes grow near Lake Erie.

Many Pennsylvanians work in manufacturing. Food processing has long been an important industry in the state. Chocolate and cocoa are leading products, as well as ice cream and canned mushrooms.

Jobs in service industries are growing rapidly. Services employ about three-fourths of the nonfarm labor force. Some of the key service areas are entertainment, health care, and retail sales.

I DIDN'T KNOW THAT!

Milk is the official state beverage. Pennsylvania is one of the leading U.S. milk-producing states.

Railroads in Pennsylvania were essential for transporting Union troops and supplies during the Civil War. At that time, Pennsylvania had nearly 2,600 miles of railroad track, more than any other state.

Pennsylvania was the site of the country's first hospital, library, and insurance company.

Hershey Foods and H.J. Heinz are two of the state's leading food producers. Pennsylvania companies are also known for making snack foods such as pretzels and potato chips.

HEINZ 36 OZ SIZE

HEINZ
TOMATO KETCHUP
NET WT 36 OZ (2 LB 4 OZ) 1.02kg

American Indians

European settlers arriving in the Pennsylvania region encountered three major groups of American Indians. These three groups were the Delaware, Susquehanna, and Shawnee. The Delaware people lived by the Delaware River. "Delaware" was the name the Europeans gave them. The Indians called themselves the Lenape or Lenni Lenape, which means "original people." Under the pressure of expanding white settlements, the Lenape began to move west and north. Today, the Lenape live mostly in Oklahoma and Canada.

During Pontiac's War, Chief Pontiac angrily accused the British of trying to kill Indians by giving them blankets that had been exposed to smallpox. His rebellion against British rule led to several major battles between Indian and British forces in western Pennsylvania.

The Susquehanna Indians were a powerful people who lived along the Susquehanna River. Illnesses brought by settlers had a devastating impact on the group. Then, over the years, wars with the Iroquois virtually eliminated the Susquehanna. In 1763, the last 20 known members of the group were murdered by settlers who were angered by Pontiac's War, in which Indian groups fought against British control of their lands.

The Shawnee came from the west around 1690. They settled on the banks of Pennsylvania's rivers. During periods of war, the Shawnee allied themselves with either French or British troops. Over time, they were forced out of Pennsylvania and eventually settled in Oklahoma.

English colonists entering Pennsylvania from Virginia in the early 17th century were greatly impressed by the Susquehanna Indians' size and appearance.

Indians and settlers lived together peacefully in Pennsylvania for many years. Later, conflicts over European settlement of Indian lands resulted in the forced migration of many American Indian groups.

Early Indians made tools, weapons, and longhouses from wood and bark. They taught early European settlers to fish, hunt, and farm. They also showed settlers trade routes through the Pennsylvania region.

Pontiac's War erupted after Chief Pontiac of the Ottawa Indians organized many different American Indian groups in 1763–1764 to resist British rule in the Great Lakes region. The war ended in a stalemate, with neither the British nor the Indians gaining a clear victory.

Pennsylvania tradition holds that William Penn reached a peace agreement with Lenape Indians in 1682 beneath the "Treaty Elm" in the village of Shackamaxon.

Explorers

T he first European known to have entered the Pennsylvania region was an Englishman, Captain John Smith. In 1608, he traveled from Virginia up the Susquehanna River and made contact with the Susquehanna Indians. Another Englishman, Henry Hudson, sailing on behalf of the Dutch, entered Delaware Bay a year later.

Swedes were the first Europeans to establish a permanent settlement in the area. Their colony, which they called New Sweden, included parts of present-day Pennsylvania, Delaware, and New Jersey. In 1643, Johan Printz, the governor of New Sweden, established his capital at Tinicum Island, near what is now Philadelphia. Not long after, Dutch settlers took over the region and changed the name to New Netherland. By 1655, the Dutch controlled most of the area.

In 1664, under the reign of King Charles II, England took command of a region that included the Pennsylvania area. Charles gave the land to his brother James, duke of York, and the entire region was renamed New York. From this land, the Pennsylvania region was then carved out and granted to William Penn in 1681.

Timeline of Settlement

Early Exploration and Settlement

1608 Traveling up the Susquehanna River, Captain John Smith enters the Pennsylvania region and encounters the Susquehanna Indians.

1609 Henry Hudson sails the *Half Moon* into Delaware Bay.

1643 Governor Johan Printz makes Tinicum Island, near present-day Philadelphia, the capital of the New Sweden colony.

Further Colonization

1655 The Dutch take over New Sweden and make it part of their New Netherland colony.

1664 English forces seize control of the New Netherland colony and rename it New York.

1681 To repay a debt, King Charles II of England grants William Penn, a Quaker, a **charter** for Pennsylvania. Penn draws up a constitution for the new colony.

Independence and American Revolution

1776 Meeting in Philadelphia on July 4, the Continental Congress approves the Declaration of Independence.

1777–1778 Pennsylvania is an important battleground in the American Revolution. General George Washington establishes his headquarters at Valley Forge.

Statehood and Civil War

1787 Delegates meeting in Philadelphia write the U.S. Constitution. On December 12, Pennsylvania becomes the 2nd state to approve the Constitution and join the Union.

1861–1865 Strongly anti-slavery, Pennsylvania has a key role in the Civil War. At Gettysburg in 1863, Union troops halt a Confederate effort to invade the North.

Early Settlers

T he founder of modern-day Pennsylvania was William Penn. Born in England in 1644, Penn was the son of an admiral in the Royal Navy. King Charles II of England had borrowed a large sum of money from the admiral. A decade after the admiral's death, the king repaid the debt in 1681 by granting William Penn a charter for the land that became Pennsylvania.

Map of Settlements and Resources in Early Pennsylvania

1 Johan Printz, governor of New Sweden, established his capital at Tinicum Island in 1643. William Penn founded the city of Philadelphia in the same region in 1681.

4 Soils in southeastern Pennsylvania were excellent for growing wheat and corn, attracting Amish and Mennonite settlers to the area.

5 Commerce in early Pennsylvania relied on water transportation, especially via the Delaware, Susquehanna, and Ohio rivers.

2 The British established Pittsburgh in 1758 and began construction of Fort Pitt a year later.

6 In 1859, Titusville was the site of the nation's first commercial oil well.

3 Harrisburg was founded along the Susquehanna River in 1785 and became the capital of Pennsylvania in 1812.

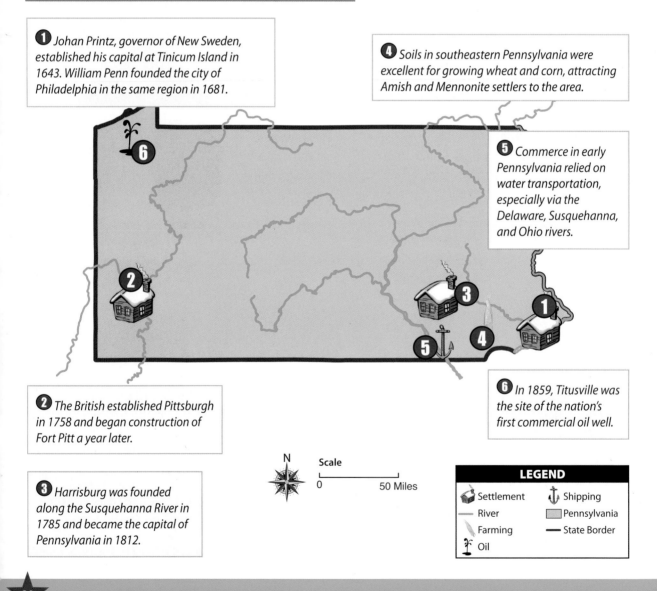

N

Scale

0   50 Miles

LEGEND

Settlement		Shipping	
— River		Pennsylvania	
Farming		— State Border	
Oil			

A religious man, Penn belonged to the Society of Friends, or Quakers. Quakers were not accepted as a religious group in England. They were **persecuted** for their beliefs and practices, which favored simplicity in speech, dress, and worship. Penn viewed the new land as a place for all people to live in peace and practice their religions. While still in England, Penn wrote the Pennsylvania Frame of Government. This constitution promised religious freedom and fair laws.

English and Welsh Quakers came to join Penn's group. They settled around Philadelphia. German settlers began cultivating the farmland in what is now commonly called "Pennsylvania Dutch" country. Many of these German immigrants were Amish and Mennonites who were attracted to the area by Penn's promise of religious freedom.

Around 1718, large numbers of Scottish and Irish people arrived. **Famine** and religious hardships in their homelands prompted them to seek new places to live. These groups colonized the Cumberland Valley. The Pennsylvania colony grew quickly as settlers from Connecticut, Maryland, and Virginia moved to the area. By 1776, on the eve of independence, Pennsylvania's population had grown to about 300,000.

I DIDN'T KNOW THAT!

William Penn called his new territory a "holy experiment" in religious freedom.

The flagship US Brig *Niagara* was built in Erie, which in the early 1800s was a small town. The *Niagara* played an important role in the War of 1812. A working replica of the *Niagara* was launched in 1990. Its home port is the Erie Maritime Museum.

In 1984, centuries after their deaths, William Penn and his wife, Hannah, were made honorary U.S. citizens.

The Continental Congress met at Independence Hall for most of the period between 1775 and 1783.

Notable People

Residents of the Keystone State have gained success as scientists, inventors, business leaders, politicians, authors, and urban planners. One remarkable Pennsylvanian, Benjamin Franklin, managed to excel in all those fields and many others, too.

BENJAMIN FRANKLIN (1706–1790)

Benjamin Franklin was one of the nation's founders. He strongly supported separation of the American colonies from Britain, was a signer the Declaration of Independence, and was a delegate to the convention that wrote the U.S. Constitution. Born in Boston, Massachusetts, he ran away to Philadelphia when he was a teenager. There he made his reputation as a writer, printer, postmaster, scientist, inventor, politician, and patriot. Franklin organized the nation's first fire department, hospital, and public lending library. Some of his inventions, such as the lighting rod, are still in use today. Franklin's portrait is displayed on the $100 bill.

JAMES BUCHANAN (1791–1868)

The only U.S. president born in Pennsylvania, James Buchanan was trained as a lawyer and spent most of his life in politics and public service. Elected to the U.S. House of Representatives and then to the Senate, he also held office as U.S. secretary of state, U.S. minister to Russia, and U.S. minister to Great Britain. As president from 1857 to 1861, he was unable to heal the divisions between North and South that led to the Civil War. Buchanan is the only president who never married. His niece, Harriet Lane, served as first lady and White House hostess during his presidency.

ANDREW W. MELLON (1855–1937)

Born in Pittsburgh, Andrew Mellon was a prominent banker and businessman. He also served as U.S. secretary of the Treasury for more than 10 years, beginning in 1921. Mellon gave generously to support charitable and educational causes in Pittsburgh and to establish the National Gallery of Art in Washington, D.C.

MARTHA GRAHAM (1894–1991)

A native of Allegheny County, Martha Graham began studying dance as a teenager. Breaking loose from ballet traditions, she pioneered a powerful style of modern dance. She founded her own dance company, which won a worldwide following. One of her most popular works was *Appalachian Spring*, with music by Aaron Copland.

MARGARET MEAD (1901–1978)

Born in Pennsylvania, Mead was in her twenties when she traveled to the Pacific Islands to study how young girls grow into adulthood. Her work there made her a pioneer in the field of anthropology, which is the study of different peoples and cultures.

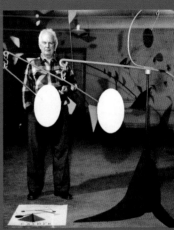

Alexander Calder (1898–1976) was one of the most influential American artists of the 20th century. Born into an artistic family in Philadelphia, he became a sculptor with a playful, colorful style. He invented the mobile, a hanging sculpture that could move with the slightest touch.

Bill Cosby (1937–) achieved success in the 1960s both as a standup comic and as a television actor. He reached the peak of his career in the 1980s with the weekly comedy series *The Cosby Show*. In 2009, he received the Mark Twain Prize for American Humor.

Population

A lthough relatively small in size, Pennsylvania ranks sixth in population among the 50 states. With more than 12.7 million residents in 2010, the Keystone State was outranked only by California, Texas, New York, Florida, and Illinois. Pennsylvania had about 283 people per square mile of land area, for a population density more than three times that of the nation as a whole.

Pennsylvania Population 1950–2010

The population of the United States has more than doubled since 1950. During the same period, Pennsylvania's population has only increased by 21 percent. What factors might account for Pennsylvania's slower growth?

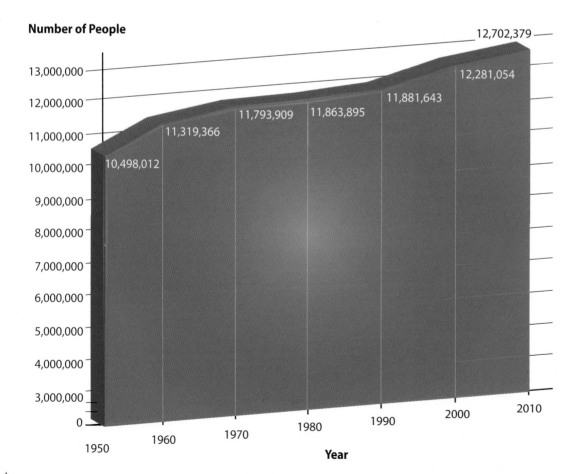

The majority of the state's citizens live in and around cities. The most populous urban area is Philadelphia. The city is the hub of a **metropolitan area** that includes more than 5.8 million people. Some of them live in the neighboring states of New Jersey, Delaware, and Maryland.

People 65 years of age or older make up a larger share of Pennsylvania's population than that of the nation as a whole. More than 15 percent of all Pennsylvanians are at least 65 years old.

Pittsburgh ranks second in population among cities in Pennsylvania. Other large cities in the state include Allentown, Erie, Reading, Bethlehem, and Scranton.

The most populous counties in Pennsylvania are Philadelphia and Allegheny counties.

African Americans account for more than 40 percent of the total population in the city of Philadelphia.

Reading is one of Pennsylvania's fastest-growing cities. Its population increased by 8.5 percent between 2000 and 2010.

The 2010 Census recorded the first population gain in 60 years for the city of Philadelphia.

Politics and Government

Pennsylvania was one of the original 13 American colonies. For much of the period between 1776 and 1800, Philadelphia served as the capital of the new nation. Laws passed during that time formed the basis of the U.S. government. From the beginning of the 19th century until the Civil War, Pennsylvania was a center of anti-slavery activity. The state also became a center of activity in support of women's rights.

The state is officially named the Commonwealth of Pennsylvania. The word "commonwealth" has its roots in a phrase meaning "the common good" or "shared well-being." Pennsylvania has had four constitutions. The present constitution came into effect in 1874.

Completed in 1906, the state capitol building in Harrisburg is a national historic landmark. Its dome rises 272 feet and weighs 52 million pounds.

Pennsylvania has three branches of government. The legislative branch, which makes the state's laws, is known as the General Assembly. It has two chambers, or parts. The upper chamber of the legislature is the Senate, with 50 members. The lower chamber is the House of Representatives, with 203 members.

The executive branch of government carries out the laws. It is headed by the governor. The governor may be elected to no more than two consecutive four-year terms. The judicial branch interprets and applies the laws. The highest court in the state is the Supreme Court, consisting of a chief justice and six other justices.

Constructed between 1871 and 1901, the Philadelphia City Hall stands 548 feet high, including the statue of William Penn at the top of the tower. It was the city's tallest building until the late 1980s.

Pennsylvania's state song is called "Pennsylvania."

Here is an excerpt from the song:

Pennsylvania, Pennsylvania
Mighty is your name,
Steeped in glory and tradition
Object of acclaim.
Where brave men fought
* the foe of freedom,*
Tyranny decried,
'Til the bell of independence
Filled the countryside.

Chorus:
Pennsylvania, Pennsylvania,
May your future be,
Filled with honor everlasting
As your history.

There are 67 counties in the state.

Wheatland, the home of President James Buchanan, is a historic building in Lancaster County.

Cultural Groups

African Americans make up more than 10 percent of the state population. Most live in cities, especially Philadelphia, Pittsburgh, and Harrisburg. Hispanic Americans account for about 5 percent of state residents, a much smaller share than in neighboring states such as New York and New Jersey. Only about four percent of all Pennsylvania residents were born in a foreign country, which is less than half the figure for the nation as a whole.

More than 50,000 Amish live in Pennsylvania today. Their beliefs are grounded in **modesty**, family, and community. Their homes do not have electricity. Amish people usually grow their own food and make their own clothing. Women and girls wear plain cotton dresses and aprons. Men and boys wear dark suits and cotton shirts. Women wear prayer caps, and men wear straw hats.

Wilson Goode was the first African American mayor of Philadelphia. He held office from 1984 to 1992.

Amish children usually attend school only through the eighth grade.

Most Amish people speak three languages. The everyday language of the Amish was originally German. After years in the United States, their language changed. Today, they speak a German **dialect** called Pennsylvania German at home. In church the Amish speak High German, a more formal version of the language. English is learned in school and is spoken whenever dealing with people outside the group.

Scandinavian culture is also represented in the state. Settlers from Scandinavia began arriving in the New World in the 1600s. The first Scandinavian settlers in Pennsylvania were the Swedes. Today, the Scandinavian Society of Western Pennsylvania promotes traditional activities in the Pittsburgh area. Celebrations include folk festivals and other cultural events. The festivals feature traditional clothing such as heavy wool jackets and vests and sometimes wooden clogs. Traditional foods such as sausages, meatballs, cheese, and flatbread are usually served at these gatherings.

I DIDN'T KNOW THAT!

Amish women do not wear jewelry.

More than 100 different religious groups live in Pennsylvania.

During the 20th century, many African Americans migrated to Pennsylvania, often from Southern states. They came because Pennsylvania offered better job opportunities.

The Goschenhoppen Folk Festival seeks to preserve German culture in Pennsylvania. It has been held annually since 1967.

The settlement called Germantown was established by German immigrants in 1683. Today it is a residential section of Philadelphia.

Arts and Entertainment

Pennsylvania's performing arts community has its own avenue to call home. The Avenue of the Arts in Philadelphia offers world-class cultural attractions. The avenue is home to ballets, operas, theaters, and concert halls. The Philadelphia Orchestra, founded in 1900, is widely regarded as one of the world's finest symphony orchestras. The city also hosts the Pennsylvania Ballet.

In western Pennsylvania, Pittsburgh is the most important cultural center. The Pittsburgh Symphony Orchestra plays its concerts in Heinz Hall. The city also has opera and dance companies. The Carnegie Museums of Pittsburgh include the Carnegie Museum of Art, Carnegie Museum of Natural History, Carnegie Science Center, and Andy Warhol Museum. Warhol, a Pittsburgh native, was one of the best-known American artists of the 20th century.

Marian Anderson gained worldwide fame as both an exceptional musician and a civil rights pioneer.

Louisa May Alcott, author of *Little Women*, was born in Germantown. Other Pennsylvania writers include the novelists James Michener and John Updike. Pulitzer Prize–winning playwright August Wilson was born in Pittsburgh. The famous Barrymore acting family came from Philadelphia, as did the celebrated comedians W. C. Fields and Bill Cosby.

One of the finest singers of the 20th century was Marian Anderson, who performed both European classical and American traditional music. Other performers and recording artists connected with Pennsylvania include Patti LaBelle, Teddy Pendergrass, Trent Reznor, Christina Aguilera, and Taylor Swift. Born and raised in the Philadelphia area, Will Smith has made a name for himself as the star of films such as *Independence Day, Men in Black, Ali*, and *Hitch*.

Taylor Swift has been named Entertainer of the Year by the Country Music Association and Artist of the Year by Billboard *magazine*.

I DIDN'T KNOW THAT!

"Philadelphia soul" or the "Philly sound" was a popular form of soul music in the 1970s. The style blended jazz, funk, and rhythm and blues, often with sophisticated string and horn arrangements.

Tina Fey has starred on television in *Saturday Night Live* and *30 Rock*. In 2010, she won the Mark Twain Prize for American Humor.

Will Smith began his career as a rapper called the Fresh Prince. He soon graduated to television, starring in the hit series *The Fresh Prince of Bel-Air.*

Sports

Sports fans in Pennsylvania have much to enjoy. Professional basketball, soccer, hockey, football, and baseball are all played in the state. The Philadelphia 76ers play in the National Basketball Association, and the Philadelphia Union competes in Major League Soccer. The National Hockey League boasts the Philadelphia Flyers and the Pittsburgh Penguins. In football, Philadelphia has the Eagles and Pittsburgh has the Steelers. Major League Baseball fields the Philadelphia Phillies and the Pittsburgh Pirates. Having more than one team per league in several pro sports makes for exciting cross-state rivalries.

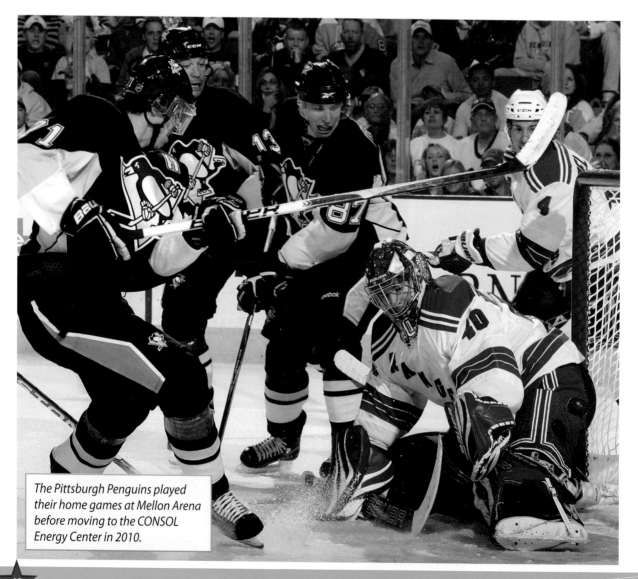

The Pittsburgh Penguins played their home games at Mellon Arena before moving to the CONSOL Energy Center in 2010.

Sporting events in Pennsylvania appeal to all age groups. Little League Baseball was founded in Williamsport in 1939 with only three teams. Today, there are thousands of Little League teams around the world. Universities and colleges throughout the state field sports teams for men and women. Almost every collegiate sport is played in the state.

Outdoor sports facilities are abundant. Among the most popular sporting activities in Pennsylvania are fishing, swimming, hiking, and golf. The Pocono Mountains and the Delaware Water Gap are two popular spots. Winter brings snow to the mountain regions, offering opportunities for skiing, snowshoeing, and sledding.

Williamsport hosts the Little League Baseball World Series every August.

I DIDN'T KNOW THAT!

Baseball slugger Reggie Jackson was born in Wyncote, near Philadelphia, in 1946.

The Philadelphia Phillies are the oldest professional sports team to have kept the same name and the same city throughout their entire history.

The Pittsburgh Steelers won four Super Bowls in six years, from 1975 through 1980.

Sidney Crosby, the captain of the Pittsburgh Penguins, is one of today's superstars in pro hockey.

Golfing greats Betsy King and Arnold Palmer are both Pennsylvania natives.

National Averages Comparison

The United States is a federal republic, consisting of fifty states and the District of Columbia. Alaska and Hawai'i are the only non-contiguous, or non-touching, states in the nation. Today, the United States of America is the third-largest country in the world in population. The United States Census Bureau takes a census, or count of all the people, every ten years. It also regularly collects other kinds of data about the population and the economy. How does Pennsylvania compare to the national average?

Comparison Chart

United States 2010 Census Data *	USA	Pennsylvania
Admission to Union	NA	December 12, 1787
Land Area (in square miles)	3,537,438.44	44,816.61
Population Total	308,745,538	12,702,379
Population Density (people per square mile)	87.28	283.43
Population Percentage Change (April 1, 2000, to April 1, 2010)	9.7%	3.4%
White Persons (percent)	72.4%	81.9%
Black Persons (percent)	12.6%	10.8%
American Indian and Alaska Native Persons (percent)	0.9%	0.2%
Asian Persons (percent)	4.8%	2.7%
Native Hawaiian and Other Pacific Islander Persons (percent)	0.2%	—
Some Other Race (percent)	6.2%	2.4%
Persons Reporting Two or More Races (percent)	2.9%	1.9%
Persons of Hispanic or Latino Origin (percent)	16.3%	5.7%
Not of Hispanic or Latino Origin (percent)	83.7%	94.3%
Median Household Income	$52,029	$50,702
Percentage of People Age 25 or Over Who Have Graduated from High School	80.4%	81.9%

*All figures are based on the 2010 United States Census, with the exception of the last two items. Percentages may not add to 100 because of rounding.

How to Improve My Community

Strong communities make strong states. Think about what features are important in your community. What do you value? Education? Health? Forests? Safety? Beautiful spaces? Government works to help citizens create ideal living conditions that are fair to all by providing services in communities. Consider what changes you could make in your community. How would they improve your state as a whole? Using this concept web as a guide, write a report that outlines the features you think are most important in your community and what improvements could be made. A strong state needs strong communities.

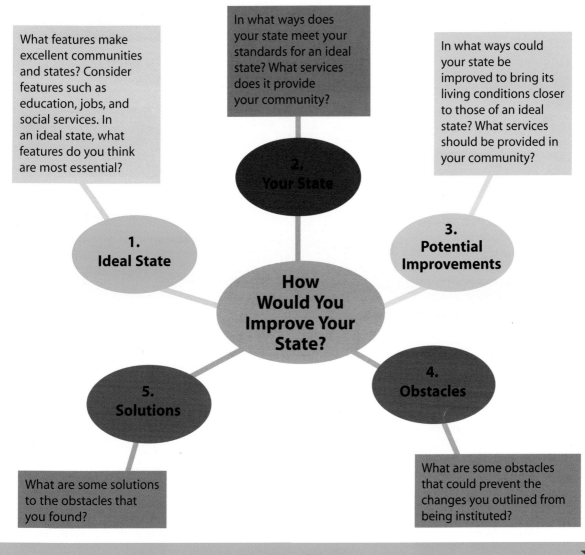

What features make excellent communities and states? Consider features such as education, jobs, and social services. In an ideal state, what features do you think are most essential?

In what ways does your state meet your standards for an ideal state? What services does it provide your community?

In what ways could your state be improved to bring its living conditions closer to those of an ideal state? What services should be provided in your community?

2.
Your State

3.
Potential Improvements

1.
Ideal State

How Would You Improve Your State?

4.
Obstacles

5.
Solutions

What are some solutions to the obstacles that you found?

What are some obstacles that could prevent the changes you outlined from being instituted?

Exercise Your Mind!

Think about these questions and then use your research skills to find the answers and learn more fascinating facts about Pennsylvania. A teacher, librarian, or parent may be able to help you locate the best sources to use in your research.

1 Independence Hall was more than the first place of government. What other purpose did it once serve?

2 After it was remade in the 1700s, when did the Liberty Bell crack again?

3 What Pennsylvania woodchuck has famous friends?

4 Pennsylvania was given to William Penn from King Charles II as payment for a debt. How much did the king owe him?

5 What is the biggest natural lake in the state?

6 What cost $110,168.05 to build in 1791?

7 What Pennsylvania city is nicknamed "Christmas City"?

8 Pennsylvania is known as the Keystone State. What other nickname does the state have?

Words to Know

charter: a legal document, often issued by the head of a state or country, granting certain rights and privileges to someone else

dialect: any special variety of a language

estuary: the part of a river where it meets the sea and where fresh and salt water mix

famine: widespread hunger

hydroelectric power: electricity produced by using the force of moving water

metropolitan area: a large city and its surrounding suburbs

modesty: not showing off oneself or one's talents

persecuted: attacked for one's beliefs

reforestation: replanting trees to replace those cut down

rural: relating to the countryside, as opposed to the city

urban: relating to the city, as opposed to the countryside

Index

American Indians 26, 27, 28, 29

American Revolution 20, 29

Amish 5, 20, 30, 31, 38, 39

Anderson, Marian 40, 41

Buchanan, James 32, 37

Calder, Alexander 33

Civil War 5, 21, 23, 25, 29, 32, 36

coal 15

Cosby, Bill 33, 40

Declaration of Independence 4, 29, 32

Delaware River 6, 10, 26

Fey, Tina 41

Franklin, Benjamin 32

Gettysburg 5, 20, 21, 29

Graham, Martha 33

Groundhog Day 12

Harrisburg 8, 9, 30, 36, 38

Independence Hall 4, 31

Lake Erie 6, 8, 10, 13, 25

Lenape Indians 26, 28

Liberty Bell 20, 21

Little League Baseball 43

Mead, Margaret 33

Mellon, Andrew W. 33

natural gas 15

Ohio River 11, 30

oil 15, 30

Pennsylvania Turnpike 6, 7

Penn, William 4, 28, 29, 30, 31, 37

Philadelphia 4, 5, 6, 7, 9, 10, 13, 20, 21, 23, 28, 29, 30, 31, 32, 33, 35, 36, 37, 38, 39, 40, 41, 42, 43

Pittsburgh 5, 7, 11, 30, 33, 35, 38, 39, 40, 42, 43

Pontiac's War 26, 27

Punxsutawney Phil 12

Quakers 4, 29, 31

Scranton 35

Shawnee Indians 26, 27

Smith, Will 41

steel 22, 23

Susquehanna Indians 27, 28, 29

Susquehanna River 9, 10, 27, 28, 29, 30

Titusville 15, 30

U.S. Constitution 4, 29, 32

Valley Forge 20, 29

Washington, George 20, 21, 29

Log on to www.av2books.com

AV² by Weigl brings you media enhanced books that support active learning. Go to www.av2books.com, and enter the special code found on page 2 of this book. You will gain access to enriched and enhanced content that supplements and complements this book. Content includes video, audio, web links, quizzes, a slide show, and activities.

Audio
Listen to sections of the book read aloud.

Video
Watch informative video clips.

Embedded Weblinks
Gain additional information for research.

Try This!
Complete activities and hands-on experiments.

WHAT'S ONLINE?

Try This!	Embedded Weblinks	Video	EXTRA FEATURES
Test your knowledge of the state in a mapping activity.	Discover more attractions in Pennsylvania.	Watch a video introduction to Pennsylvania.	**Audio** Listen to sections of the book read aloud.
Find out more about precipitation in your city.	Learn more about the history of the state.	Watch a video about the features of the state.	**Key Words** Study vocabulary, and complete a matching word activity.
Plan what attractions you would like to visit in the state.	Learn the full lyrics of the state song.		**Slide Show** View images and captions, and prepare a presentation.
Learn more about the early natural resources of the state.			**Quizzes** Test your knowledge.
Write a biography about a notable resident of Pennsylvania.			
Complete an educational census activity.			

AV² was built to bridge the gap between print and digital. We encourage you to tell us what you like and what you want to see in the future.
Sign up to be an AV² Ambassador at www.av2books.com/ambassador.